# Fasting
A Haven from Hellfire

# Fasting

A Haven from Hellfire

According to the Rulings of
Grand Ayatullah Sayyid Ali al-Husseini al-Sistani

Imam Mahdi Association of Marjaeya

Imam Mahdi Association of Marjaeya, Dearborn,
MI 48124, www.imam-us.org
© 2016, 2020 by Imam Mahdi Association of Marjaeya
All rights reserved.
First edition 2016. Second edition 2020.
Printed in the United States of America

ISBN-978-0-9997877-4-8

No part of this publication may be reproduced without permission from I.M.A.M., except in cases of fair use. Brief quotations, especially for the purpose of propagating Islamic teachings, are allowed.

# Contents

I.M.A.M.'s Foreword ................................................... ix
Endorsement from the Office of
His Eminence in Najaf ............................................. xiii

1. **Fasting in the Month of Ramadan in Islam** ........ 1
   Fasting in the Month of Ramadan in the Holy
   Quran ............................................................................ 2
   Fasting in the Month of Ramadan in the Sunnah .... 3

2. **Types of Fasts** ....................................................... 7
   Four Types of Fasts ..................................................... 8
     Obligatory fasts ........................................................ 8
     Forbidden fasts ........................................................ 8
     Detested fasts .......................................................... 9
     Recommended fasts ................................................ 9
     Questions ............................................................... 10

3. **Who Must Fast in the Month of Ramadan?** ...... 15
   One Who Has Reached the Age of Religious
   Obligation (Bulugh) ................................................... 16
     Girls ........................................................................ 16
     Boys ........................................................................ 16
     Questions ............................................................... 17
   One Who Is Sane ........................................................ 18
   One Who Is Conscious .............................................. 18
     Questions ............................................................... 18
   A Woman Who Is Free from Menstrual and Post-
   Partum Bleeding ........................................................ 19
     Questions ............................................................... 19
   One Who Will Not Be Harmed by Fasting ............... 20
     Harm to one's health ............................................. 20

Contents

    Other harm..................................................................20
    Questions....................................................................21
  One Who Will Not Experience Extreme Hardship
  by Fasting..........................................................................25
  One Who Is Not Traveling..................................................26
    Questions....................................................................26
  One Who Will Not Experience Harm or Extreme
  Hardship Because of Old Age............................................29
    Questions....................................................................29
  One Who Is Not Suffering from Polydipsia.....................29

4. **How Do We Fast in the Month of Ramadan?.... 31**
    Questions....................................................................32
  The Eight Fast-Nullifiers to Avoid ..................................33
    First and second: Eating and drinking..................34
    Third: Intercourse ..................................................36
    Fourth: Masturbation ............................................36
    Fifth: Vomiting .......................................................37
    Sixth: Liquid enema ...............................................37
    Seventh: Ascribing lies to Allah, His messenger,
      or the infallible Imams .........................................37
    Eighth: Allowing heavy dust or smoke to enter
      the throat ................................................................39
    Questions....................................................................39

5. **When Does the Month of Ramadan Begin and
End? ................................................................................ 45**
  The Beginning and Ending of the Lunar Month ...46
  Proving the Presence of the Crescent Moon on
  the Horizon.......................................................................46

6. **Rulings About Disrupting the Fast in
the Month of Ramadan.................................................. 53**
  Fast Disruption Type 1 .....................................................54
  Fast Disruption Type 2 .....................................................54
    Questions....................................................................54

## Contents

Fast Disruption Type 3 .................. 58
    Questions .................................. 59
Fast Disruption Type 4 .................. 61
    Questions .................................. 62
In Closing ...................................... 65
Appendix ........................................ 67
Important Documents about Horizon and Astronomical Data ........................ 67
Document 1: Questions and Answers regarding the First Day of Shawwal 1428 AH ............ 68
Document 2: The Horizon in the School of al-Sayyid al-Sistani ................................ 73
Document 3: The Horizon Criteria and Advice ...... 77
Document 4: A Practical Example .......... 82
Glossary ........................................ 85

# I.M.A.M.'s Foreword

In the name of Almighty Allah

May Allah shower His peace and blessings upon Prophet Muhammad and his holy progeny

Imam Jafar al-Sadiq (p) is reported to have said, "Nothing but three things rectify a Muslim: a deeper understanding of religion, patience upon a misfortune, and good economizing of living expenses."[1] Fasting is one of the most important duties in Islam, in addition to prayer and other obligatory requirements. Hence, it is imperative for one to fully understand its rulings to ensure they are properly discharged. Fasting is one of the most important acts of worship that enhances and elevates a person physically, spiritually, and socially. Thus, fasting touches on many aspects of our individual and social life. Hence, a prudent person should thank God, the Exalted, for this grace and strive to learn the fundamentals of fasting, understand its implications, be mindful of its intricacies, and practice it in the best way. The key to all this is to learn its jurisprudence.

---

1. Shaykh al-Kulayni, *Al-kafi*, vol. 5, p. 87.: "لا يُصلح المرء المسلم إلا ثلاثة التفقّه في الدّين والصّبر على النائبة وحسن التقدير في المعيشة"

## I.M.A.M.'s Foreword

Accordingly, I.M.A.M. presents the second edition of this booklet, which is a reformulation of the first edition (2016). It contains additional information and is more precisely written after a comprehensive review.

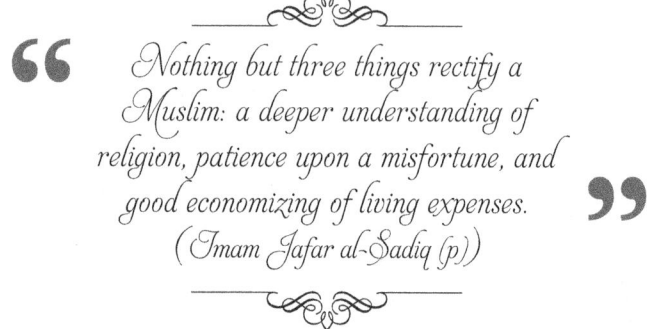

> *Nothing but three things rectify a Muslim: a deeper understanding of religion, patience upon a misfortune, and good economizing of living expenses.*
> (*Imam Jafar al-Sadiq (p)*)

As mentioned in the first edition, this book, *Fasting: A Haven from Hellfire*, is a translation of the Arabic version *Al-siyamu junnatun min al-nar* (Arabic: الصّيام جُنّة من النار).[2] An electronic version is also available on the website of the Office of the Supreme Religious Authority of His Eminence Grand Ayatullah Sayyid al-Sistani (may God prolong his life).[3] It highlights the rulings of this important and obligatory act enacted by God in the blessed month of Ramadan, the month the Holy Quran was revealed. We found it necessary to clarify some of the complicated phrases in the first edition and add explanations, sources, and comments to the existing content given the way the book was compiled and

---

2. This phrase is from an honorable tradition narrated by the Prophet (pbuh&hp) in a holy narration by Imam al-Sadiq (p) and found in several sources, such as Al-kafi by Shaykh al-Kulayni, vol. 4, p. 62.

3. https://www.sistani.org/downloads/siam.pdf.

presented. It was also necessary to add an appendix of some important edicts, such as the rulings of establishing the crescent and multiplicity of horizons from *Minhaj al-salihin, Al-taliqa ala al-urwat al-wuthqa,* and *Al-masail al-muntakhabah,* in addition to what was published in the Questions and Answers section on the website of His Eminence's Office.

Moreover, religious learning material requires translating and accurate explanation, especially for practical rulings that are sometimes complicated and challenging to decipher. Therefore, the first edition had to be precisely reviewed and made more complete with addendums, explanations, and clarifications. As such, this version is a revision and reformulation of the translated text, which was then reverified for its conformity to the original Arabic version. We hope in God, the Exalted, that we succeeded in making it easy to understand and useful for believers in performing their fasts. Given the research method and information sequence, it is important to note that some sections of the book were rearranged to make the presentation more suitable. Thus, the glossary at the end of the book is updated and the work's design implements the style adopted by the organization in its electronic and printed publications.

We would like to thank God, the Exalted, for His kindness and support and extend our gratitude to everyone who contributed to the preparation of this book beginning with the first edition and including this second one, especially the honorable Dr. Shaykh Mehdi S. Hazari, who overwhelmed us with his continuous volunteer work and dedication of his precious time, great efforts, and work to extreme precision and a high linguistic level.

We ask the Almighty to accept this work with His gracious acceptance and to make it a source of blessing in the hereafter of all those who participated in this work.

**Sayyid M. B. Kashmiri**
Jurist's Representative

# Endorsement from the Office of His Eminence in Najaf

In the name of the Most High

After giving thanks [to Allah] and praises to the Prophet (pbuh&hp) and his Holy Household (pbut)

Verily, the dissertation entitled *Al-siyamu junnatun min al-nar*[4] corresponds to the verdicts of His Eminence Sayyid al-Sistani (may Allah prolong his life).

---

4. Translates to *Fasting: A Haven from Hellfire*. It is a hadith.

*Endorsement*

Therefore, it is permissible to act in accordance to its contents, and he who follows it will be rewarded if Allah Almighty so pleases.

The seal of the office of Sayyid al-Sistani
The Holy City of Najaf
Rajab 25, 1426

Chapter 1

# Fasting in the Month of Ramadan in Islam

## Fasting in the Month of Ramadan in the Holy Quran

﴿يَا أَيُّهَا الَّذِينَ آمَنُواْ كُتِبَ عَلَيْكُمُ الصِّيَامُ كَمَا كُتِبَ عَلَى الَّذِينَ مِن قَبْلِكُمْ لَعَلَّكُمْ تَتَّقُونَ ۝ أَيَّامًا مَّعْدُودَاتٍ فَمَن كَانَ مِنكُم مَّرِيضًا أَوْ عَلَى سَفَرٍ فَعِدَّةٌ مِّنْ أَيَّامٍ أُخَرَ وَعَلَى الَّذِينَ يُطِيقُونَهُ فِدْيَةٌ طَعَامُ مِسْكِينٍ فَمَن تَطَوَّعَ خَيْرًا فَهُوَ خَيْرٌ لَّهُ وَأَن تَصُومُواْ خَيْرٌ لَّكُمْ إِن كُنتُمْ تَعْلَمُونَ ۝ شَهْرُ رَمَضَانَ الَّذِي أُنزِلَ فِيهِ الْقُرْآنُ هُدًى لِّلنَّاسِ وَبَيِّنَاتٍ مِّنَ الْهُدَى وَالْفُرْقَانِ فَمَن شَهِدَ مِنكُمُ الشَّهْرَ فَلْيَصُمْهُ وَمَن كَانَ مَرِيضًا أَوْ عَلَى سَفَرٍ فَعِدَّةٌ مِّنْ أَيَّامٍ أُخَرَ يُرِيدُ اللَّهُ بِكُمُ الْيُسْرَ وَلاَ يُرِيدُ بِكُمُ الْعُسْرَ وَلِتُكْمِلُواْ الْعِدَّةَ وَلِتُكَبِّرُواْ اللَّهَ عَلَى مَا هَدَاكُمْ وَلَعَلَّكُمْ تَشْكُرُونَ﴾

O believers, fasting has been made mandatory for you as it was made mandatory for the people before you, so that you may have fear of Allah.

Fasting is only for a certain number of days. One who is sick or on a journey has to fast the same number of days at another time. Those who can afford redemption should feed a poor person. Good deeds performed on one's own initiative will be rewarded. However, fasting is better and will be rewarded. Would that you had known this!

The month of Ramadan is the month in which the Quran was revealed; a guide for the people, the most authoritative of all guidance and a criterion to discern right from wrong. Anyone of you who knows that the month of Ramadan has begun must start to fast. Those who are sick or who are on a journey have to fast the same number of days at another time. Allah does not impose any hardship upon you. He wants you to have comfort so that you may complete the fast, glorify Allah for His having given you guidance, and perhaps you give Him thanks.[5]

## Fasting in the Month of Ramadan in the Sunnah

جاءَ في خِطْبَةِ النَّبِيِّ الأكرم (صَلَّى اللهُ عَلَيْهِ وَآلِهِ) في آخِرِ جُمُعَةٍ مِنْ شَهْرِ شَعْبَانَ:

"أَيُّهَا النَّاسُ إِنَّهُ قَدْ أَقْبَلَ إِلَيْكُمْ شَهْرُ اللهِ بِالْبَرَكَةِ وَالرَّحْمَةِ وَالْمَغْفِرَةِ. شَهْرٌ هُوَ عِنْدَ اللهِ أَفْضَلُ الشُّهُورِ، وَأَيَّامُهُ أَفْضَلُ الأَيَّامِ، وَلَيَالِيهِ أَفْضَلُ اللَّيَالِي، وَسَاعَاتُهُ أَفْضَلُ السَّاعَاتِ. هُوَ شَهْرٌ دُعِيتُمْ فِيهِ إِلَى ضِيَافَةِ اللهِ، وَجُعِلْتُمْ فِيهِ مِنْ أَهْلِ كَرَامَةِ اللهِ. أَنْفَاسُكُمْ فِيهِ تَسْبِيحٌ، وَنَوْمُكُمْ فِيهِ عِبَادَةٌ، وَعَمَلُكُمْ فِيهِ مَقْبُولٌ، وَدُعَاؤُكُمْ فِيهِ مُسْتَجَابٌ، فَاسْأَلُوا اللهَ رَبَّكُمْ بِنِيَّاتٍ صَادِقَةٍ، وَقُلُوبٍ طَاهِرَةٍ، أَنْ يُوَفِّقَكُمْ لِصِيَامِهِ، وَتِلَاوَةِ كِتَابِهِ، فَإِنَّ الشَّقِيَّ مَنْ حُرِمَ غُفْرَانَ اللهِ فِي هَذَا الشَّهْرِ الْعَظِيمِ".

---

5. The Holy Quran 2:183–185. All Quranic quotations in this booklet are from the Muhammad Sarwar translation.

## Fasting: A Haven from Hellfire

A part of the Prophet's sermon at the end of Shaban: "O People! Surely the month of Allah has approached you with blessings, mercy, and forgiveness. It is a month that is to Allah the best of months, its days the best of days, its nights the best of nights, and its hours the best of hours. It is a month in which you have been invited to be hosted by Allah, and in it you have been made of those who are worthy to be in the grace of Allah. Your breaths in it are exaltation, your deeds in it are accepted, and your supplications in it are answered. Therefore, ask Allah with true intentions and pure hearts that he make you successful in fasting it and in reciting His Book. For only the deviant is the one who is deprived of the forgiveness of Allah in this great month."[6]

وقالَ رسولُ الله (ص): "مَنْ صَامَ شَهْرَ رَمَضان إِيْماناً وَاحْتِساباً غَفَرَ اللهُ مَا تَقَدَّمَ مِنْ ذَنْبِهِ".

The Messenger of Allah (pbuh&hp) said, "He who fasts the month of Ramadan out of belief and dependence, then Allah will forgive his past sins."[7]

وقالَ (ص): "الصِّيامُ جُنَّةُ العَبْدِ الْمُؤْمِنِ يومَ القيامةِ كما يَقي أَحَدُكُم سِلاحَه في الدنيا".

---

6. Shaykh al-Majlisi, *Bihar al-anwar*, vol. 93, p. 356.

7. Shaykh al-Saduq, *Fadail al-ashhur al-thalatha*, p. 105, and *Bihar al-anwar*, vol. 97, p. 34.

"Fasting is a believing worshipper's protection on the Day of Judgment, just as one of you would protect his weapon in this world."[8]

وقالَ (ص): "مَنْ صَامَ شَهْرَ رَمَضانَ فَاجْتَنَبَ فيهِ الحرامَ والبُهْتانَ رَضِيَ اللهُ عَنْهُ وَأَوْجَبَ لَهُ الجِنانِ".

"He who fasted the month of Ramadan, and in doing so avoided the prohibitions and [slander], then Allah will be pleased with him and will make heaven obligatory for him."[9]

وقالَ (ص): "مَنْ مَنَعَهُ الصَّوْمُ مِنْ طَعَامٍ يَشْتَهيْه كانَ حَقّاً عَلَى اللهِ أَنْ يُطعِمَهُ مِنْ طَعَامِ الجَنَّةِ ويُسْقيهُ مِنْ شَرابِها".

"He whose fasting prevented him from food that he desires, it will be his right upon Allah that He feeds him from the food of heaven and that he is served from its drinks."[10]

وقالَ (ص): "للصَّائِمِ فَرْحَتانِ: فَرْحَةٌ عِندَ إفطارِهِ وَفَرْحَةٌ يَوْمَ يَلقى رَبَّهُ".

"A fasting person has two joys: the joy he feels at the time of breaking his fast and the joy he feels when he meets his Lord."[11]

---

8. Shaykh al-Saduq, *Fadail al-ashhur al-thalatha*, p. 134.

9. Shaykh al-Majlisi, *Bihar al-anwar*, vol. 93, p. 346.

10. Shaykh al-Majlisi, *Bihar al-anwar*, vol. 93, p. 322.

11. Shaykh al-Saduq, *Fadail al-ashhur al-thalatha*, p. 143.

## Fasting: A Haven from Hellfire

وقالَ (ص): "لِكُلِّ شَيْءٍ زَكَاة وَزَكاةُ الأَجْسَامِ الصِّيام".

"For everything there is a charity, and the charity of the bodies is fasting."[12]

وقالَ أميرُ المؤمنين (ع): "صَوْمُ شَهْرِ رَمَضَانَ جُنَّةٌ مِنَ النَّارِ".

The Master of the Faithful (p) said, "Fasting the month of Ramadan is a haven from the hellfire."[13]

وَقالَ الإمامُ الصَّادق (ع): "إنَّ الصَّائِمَ مِنْكُم لِيَرتَعَ في رِياضِ الجَنَّةِ تَدعُوا لَهُ الْمَلائِكَةُ حَتَّى يَفْطُر".

Imam al-Sadiq (p) said, "Surely the fasting person will rest in the gardens of heaven with the angels supplicating for him until he breaks his fast."[14]

وقالَ (ع): "مَنْ أَفْطَرَ يَوماً مِنْ شَهْرِ رَمَضانَ خَرَجَ رُوحُ الإيمانُ مِنْهُ".

Imam al-Sadiq (p) said, "He who breaks his fast for one day during the month of Ramadan, the Spirit of Faith shall leave him."[15]

---

12. Shaykh al-Tusi, vol. 4, p. 191.

13. Shaykh al-Majlisi, *Bihar al-anwar*, vol. 93, p. 342.

14. Shaykh al-Majlisi, *Bihar al-anwar*, vol. 27, p. 132.

15. Shaykh al-Saduq, *Man la yahthuruh al-faqih*, vol. 2, p. 118.

Chapter 2

# Types of Fasts

## Four Types of Fasts

There are four types of fasts: obligatory, forbidden, detested, and recommended.

### Obligatory fasts

Obligatory fasts are

- fasts in the month of Ramadan and its make-up fasts, which are the most important of all;
- fasts required for expiation (*kaffarah*);
- fasts made because of vows, pledges, and oaths to Allah (*nadhr, ahd,* and *yamin,* respectively); and
- hired fasts (paid for the service of performing make-up fasts on behalf of someone who is deceased).

### Forbidden fasts

Days in which fasting is forbidden include fasting

- on the first of Shawwal (Eid al-Fitr);
- on the tenth of Dhu al-Hijjah (Eid al-Adha);
- on the eleventh, twelfth, and thirteenth of Dhu al-Hijjah for those in Mina during the fulfillment of their hajj obligation;
- on the day of doubt (i.e., the thirtieth of Shaban or the first of the month of Ramadan) with the intention of it being the first of the month of Ramadan; and
- for a wife if she engages in a voluntary or undefined (i.e., recommended) fast without

the permission of her husband if it prevents him from his marital rights.
- By obligatory precaution,[16] the wife may not fast a voluntary fast if her husband forbids her, even if it does not affect the fulfillment of his marital rights with her.

## Detested fasts

Detested fasts include, but are not exclusive to, fasting

- on the ninth of Dhu al-Hijjah (Day of Arafah) for those afraid that fasting will weaken them so much that they will not be able to engage in supplication;
- for a guest to engage in a voluntary or undefined (i.e., recommended) fast without the permission of the host; and
- for a child, voluntarily, without the permission of their father.

## Recommended fasts

Fasting is recommended on any day of the remaining days of the year other than the obligatory, forbidden, or detested days. Some days are more recommended for fasting than others. For example, fasting in the months of Rajab and Shaban is better than fasting in other months. Recommended fasts are permissible for those who fulfill the following conditions:

---

16. This is a ruling that is obligatory to follow based on precaution. According to Sayyid al-Sistani, in such verdicts, one may follow the next most knowledgeable jurist after him.

## Fasting: A Haven from Hellfire

- Fasting does not cause health-related harm.
- One is not a traveler (i.e., those who must pray *qasr* or shortened prayers), except fasting three days in Medina to beseech God to fulfill a need with the condition that the fasts are on Wednesday, Thursday, and Friday consecutively based on obligatory precaution.
- For a woman, she must not be menstruating (*haydh*) or have post-partum bleeding (*nifas*).
- One does not have make-up fasts from previous month(s) of Ramadan because those have priority.
  - Recommended fasts are allowed [before performing make-up fasts of kaffarah, nadhr, and the like] if those other obligatory fasts still need to be made up.

## Questions

Q: If one must make up a fast from the month of Ramadan, is it permissible for them to fast on behalf of a deceased person either voluntarily or as a paid fast?

A: Only for an obligatory fast of the deceased (such as a missed fast from the month of Ramadan) but not for their recommended fasts. One's make-up fasts from Ramadan take precedence over their recommended fasts irrespective of whether they are paid or unpaid (i.e., voluntary).

## Types of Fasts

Q: How does one fast a recommended fast?

A: Recommended fasts do not differ from obligatory fasts for the month of Ramadan except in the following ways:

- The intention may be delayed to just before sunset if one did not partake of any fast-nullifiers—even if they intended to break their fast during the day but did not.
- Staying in *janabah* intentionally until *fajr* (dawn) does not prevent one from fasting a recommended fast during the day. For example, if a person becomes *mujnib* (in a state of janabah) at night and then wants to fast a recommended fast the next day, they do not have to do *ghusl* (major ablution) before dawn (fajr) for the fast to be valid.
- A person fasting a recommended fast may break their fast any time before or after *dhuhr* (zenith) without consequence.
- It is not appropriate for a traveler to perform a recommended fast (e.g., first three days of Shaban). However, in case one was traveling and they did not partake of a fast nullifier during the day and came back to their land even a few minutes before *maghrib* time, they can make an intention to perform a recommended fast by completing the rest of that day, even if it is just a matter of minutes. On the other hand, it is not appropriate for the traveler to make the intention (*niyyah*) if they are traveling, even if they are sure they will be arriving home before maghrib.

Q: A person may make a nadhr to fast a day or more in thanks to God, as an example. In such a case, a general recommended fast of gratitude would become an obligatory fast to fulfill the vow. Does the fast then have special rules that differ from the recommended fast?

A: Yes. Of those rules are the following:

- If one makes a nadhr to fast a specific day, it is obligatory for them to make the intention by dawn of that day.
- If someone conducts a specified nadhr (*muayyan*) fast, they may not break their fast, even before the zenith. However, if it was an unspecified nadhr (*ghayr muayyan*) fast, they may break their fast any time before or after the zenith and fast another day.
- The person who has the nadhr fast is not required to have the intention that they want to fulfill the nadhr. It is enough for the person to intend to fast for the purpose of seeking closeness to Allah (swt). However, if their nadhr is to fast in thanks to Allah (swt) for example, then it is obligatory for them to intend to give thanks to Allah by fasting.
- If the day is specified for the nadhr fast, the person can travel that day and is then excused from the fast. However, they must make up the fast.
- A recommended fast is not valid when traveling. However, if a person intends their nadhr fast to be
    - on a specific day that they are traveling, then the nadhr is valid and the person must fast that day; or

- on a specific day, whether they are a resident or a traveler, then the fast while traveling is valid.

If a traveler wants to make the intention of a nadhr fast while they are traveling, they must do so before dawn (fajr).

Chapter 3

# Who Must Fast in the Month of Ramadan?

Fasting is obligatory for those who fulfill the following criteria:

- Have reached the age of religious obligation (*bulugh*)
- Are sane
- Are conscious
- For women, are free from menstrual (haydh) and post-partum bleeding (nifas)
- Will not be harmed by fasting
- Will not experience extreme hardship by fasting
- Are not traveling
- Will not experience harm or extreme hardship because of old age

## One Who Has Reached the Age of Religious Obligation (Bulugh)

### Girls

It is obligatory for girls to fast upon completion of nine lunar years (eight years, eight months, and twenty-one days in the solar calendar).

### Boys

It is obligatory for boys to fast when one of the following conditions is fulfilled, either

- upon the completion of fifteen lunar years;[17] or
- before the completion of fifteen lunar years if one

---

17. Fourteen years and two months in a solar calendar.

- has the growth of thick pubic hair over the male genitalia; or
- has experienced the ejaculation of semen while asleep or awake.

## Questions

Q: What about those who have not reached bulugh?

A: It is not obligatory for them to fast in the month of Ramadan. However, if they do fast, they will be rewarded.

Q: What if the person who is not *baligh* is unable to continue fasting the entire day? May they fast part of the day?

A: Yes, it is recommended to refrain from eating half of the day or more, or even less, according to what is bearable, so that the child may become accustomed to fasting.

Q: If one becomes baligh before morning prayer, is one required to fast?

A: Yes

Q: If one becomes baligh after morning prayer, is one required to fast that day?

A: No, although they must make it up and fast the following days.

## One Who Is Sane

It is not obligatory for a person to fast who becomes insane,[18] even for part of the day.

## One Who Is Conscious

Fasting is not obligatory for a person who has been unconscious for the entire day. For example, this would include someone in a coma or a person who is deeply sedated and not merely sleeping.

### Questions

Q: What if a person becomes unconscious for part of the day?

A: There are two situations here:

- If the person made the intention to fast before fajr, became unconscious thereafter, but then regained consciousness during the day, the rule is that they must continue fasting the rest of the day based on obligatory precaution. If the person does not keep the rest of the fast after regaining consciousness, they must make it up later based on obligatory precaution.
- If the person did not make the intention to fast before fajr and became unconscious, the rule is that there is no fast for them, even if they regain consciousness during the day. Moreover, no qada (make-up) is required.

---

18. One who is unable to mentally fathom the religious obligation upon them or understand how to fulfill it.

## A Woman Who Is Free from Menstrual and Post-Partum Bleeding

A woman must be pure (free from menstrual [haydh] and post-partum bleeding [nifas]) during the entirety of the day.

There are two cases here:

- If the menstrual or post-partum bleeding stops after the time for morning prayer, she does not have to fast but needs to make it up.
- If the menstrual cycle of a fasting woman starts or she sees post-partum bleeding during the day or even slightly before sunset, her fast becomes void and she needs to make it up later.

## Questions

Q: If she sees bleeding before sunset and continues fasting until sunset, is her fast accepted?

A: No, and it is not permissible for her to continue to refrain from eating the rest of the day with the intention of fasting.

Q: What is the ruling regarding the fasting of women who use birth control pills to control their menstrual cycle so that they may fast the blessed month uninterrupted?

A: It is permissible with the condition that it does not cause them grave harm.

Q: What if she saw some light bleeding in the days of her menstrual cycle despite using birth control pills?

A: If the blood was intermittent and it did not have the characteristics of the blood of menstruation, she may continue fasting in such a state.

## One Who Will Not Be Harmed by Fasting

It is not obligatory to fast if harm will result (i.e., harm that reasonable people avoid because it is rational to do so, and because the harm would be unacceptable and intolerable). It is of two types—harm to one's health and other forms.

### Harm to one's health

This includes several cases:

- If fasting causes an illness, whether it shows actual symptoms (e.g., fever and headache) or not
- If a person is ill and fasting worsens their condition
- If a person is sick and fasting delays their wellness
- If a person is sick and fasting causes them to be afflicted with another sickness, or leads the symptoms of their current illness to (re)appear or the condition to worsen (e.g., such as an increase in their temperature).

### Other harm

This is any harm to the self, family, or wealth that reasonable people would consider to be unacceptable. For example, an oppressor threatens a person with physical harm or imprisonment if they fast in the month of Ramadan.

## Questions

Q: Does the condition that revokes the obligation of fasting need to be a specifically confirmed harm or does it include unconfirmed harm?

A: It includes both. However, it is a criterion that the unconfirmed harm be probable to a degree that causes fear within the person. As for an unconfirmed harm that is very low in probability such that it does not cause fear within the person, it does not revoke the obligation of fasting.

Q: What is the ruling for a person who does not care about the harm that may result from fasting and does so anyway, holding themselves responsible for any harm that may result?

A: If the harm is to the person's health, then the fast is invalid. If the harm is not to their health, then the fast is valid.

Note: One may sin in some cases by doing so—for example, fasting that results in extreme harm, which is Islamically forbidden.

Q: What about a patient whose doctor has imposed a specific dietary and medical regimen that prevents them from fasting?

A: If leaving such a regimen will cause harm, as described previously, then it is permissible to break the fast.

Q: What about a pregnant woman whose fetus may be harmed, although she will not be harmed herself?

A: She does not have to fast. The same applies if she herself were to be harmed from fasting. And in both cases (i.e., if either she or the fetus were to be harmed)

- if she was near delivery (i.e., months eight and nine),
  - she needs to make up the fast.
  - Penance: Yes (*fidyah*: 0.75 kg of food for each day missed); and
- if she was not near delivery (e.g., until the seventh month)
  - she needs to make up the fast.
  - Penance: No.[19]

Q: What if fasting causes a decrease in breast milk for a nursing woman and results in harm to her nursing baby?

A: She does not have to fast (the same applies if she herself were to be harmed).[20]

- She needs to make up the fast.
- Penance: Yes (fidyah)

Q: If she was able to nurse using other means without harm to the baby, may she still be excused from fasting?

A: It is not permissible by obligatory precaution.[20]

---

19. If she makes it up before the next month of Ramadan; otherwise she must pay kaffarah.

20. In the case of a nursing mother who can feed her child by other means, such as using baby formula, she may not break her fast based on obligatory precaution.

## Who Must Fast in the Month of Ramadan?

Q: What if a person is ill but fasting would not cause them any complications?

A: It is obligatory to fast.

Q: If one fasts believing that their health will not be harmed, however after fasting, they were indeed harmed [by the fasting], is their fast valid?

A: Their fast is invalid by obligatory precaution.

- They need to make up the fast.
- Penance: No

Q: If one fasts believing that their health will be harmed however it is not, what is the ruling regarding their fast?

A: There are two cases here:

- If they are ignorant of the rules, and their intention of fasting was to seek nearness to Allah, the fast is valid.
- If they know the rule, then they should not do so with an intention of seeking closeness to God. The fast in such a case is invalid, and they must make up the fast.

Q: If one does not fast thinking that they will be harmed, but really they would not have been harmed, what is the ruling?

A: They must make up the fast, and there is no penance.

Q: If a person is sick during the start of the day, they are excused from fasting. However, if they become well before the end of the day, and they did not break their fast with a fast-nullifier, what is the ruling?

There are two cases here:

- The ruling is that if they become well before the zenith, by obligatory precaution, they should make the intention and fast.
  - They need to make up the fast.
  - Penance: No (unless the person does not make up the fast before the next month of Ramadan)
- The ruling is that if they become well after the zenith, they do not fast.
  - They need to make up the fast.
  - Penance: No

Q: If a person feels healthy and does not fear any harm from fasting, but the doctor has forbidden them from fasting and made them fear the consequences of it, are they required to follow the advice of the doctor?

A: No, unless a true fear of harm is instilled in them.

Q: If a person fears that fasting will harm their health, but the doctor assured them that they would not be harmed from fasting, are they required to follow the advice of the doctor?

A: No, they do not have to follow the advice of the doctor. They may refrain from fasting provided they are not being obsessive to a degree that reasonable people would consider irrational.

## One Who Will Not Experience Extreme Hardship by Fasting

Fasting should not cause extreme hardship that is unbearable according to reasonable and rational behavior. For example:

- A person who was ill and is now well but still suffers from great weakness and finds extreme hardship in fasting during their recovery is excused from fasting.
- Fasting prevents one from working because it causes weakness that is unbearable during work—it may cause unbearable thirst or other reasons. In this case,
    - one should get another job that allows one to fast; or
    - one should stop working during the month of Ramadan and depend on savings, a loan, or some other means.

Note:
- If one can do either of the above, then fasting is obligatory.
- If not, they do not have to fast on those days. However, it is an obligatory precaution that they consume the bare minimum (i.e., only so much that gives them enough energy to continue working without hardship). They must make up the fast whenever they are able to.

## One Who Is Not Traveling

Islamic domicile (*al-watan al-shari*):[21] Fasting does not apply (i.e., it is not permissible except in certain specific circumstances) to a person who prays qasr (shortened prayer) because they are away from their domicile and are considered a traveler.

## Questions

Q: What is the ruling for a traveler who does not pray qasr, such as a person who intends to stay in a place that is not their home for ten days, is a frequent traveler,[22] is traveling for purposes that are prohibited by Islam [to commit a disobedience], or travels to one place for thirty days or more and is unsure about staying (i.e., they had no prior plan to do so) there each of those days and does so in intervals of fewer than ten days [nine or fewer]?

A: It is obligatory for them to fast.

Q: If a traveler—other than those previously described—wants to fast, may they do so?

A: There are two cases here:

---

21. Islamic domicile or al-watan al-shari is a place that a person considers their home. This is either where they were born, where they live permanently, or plan to reside for ten days or more.

22. One who travels no less than ten times over the span of ten days or one who is a traveler for no less than ten days out of a month, even if the trips are [just] two or three and there is a resolve that this will continue for six months over the span of one year or over the span of three months over two years.

- If one has knowledge of the ruling [that their fast would be invalid if they fasted],
    - the fast is invalid; and
    - they must make up the fast.
- If one is ignorant of the ruling until maghrib,
    - the fast is valid; and
    - they do not need to make up the fast.

Q: If one travels during the day, what is the ruling?

A: There are two cases here:

- If they travel before the zenith and do not return before the zenith,
    - the fast is invalid; and
    - they must make up the fast.
- If they travel after the zenith,
    - the fast is valid by obligatory precaution; and
    - they do not need to make up the fast.

Q: If one arrives at their hometown or at a town where they intend to stay ten days or more during the day, what is the ruling?

A: There are two cases here:

- If they partake of a fast-nullifier during their travel,
    - the fast is invalid, and
    - they must make up the fast.
- If they do not partake of a fast-nullifier during travel and arrive [at their hometown or at a place where they are staying ten days or more]
    - before the zenith.

- they make the intention to fast when they arrive at the place, and not before, and fast; and
- they do not need to make up the fast.
  - after the zenith,
    - they are not required to fast; in fact, it is not proper to fast under these conditions based on obligatory precaution; and
    - they must make up the fast.

Q: If a traveler was at home during morning prayer and then travels in the morning and returns before the zenith of the same day without partaking of a fast-nullifier, must the traveler make the intention to fast that day when they return?

A: Yes, they should make the intention based on obligatory precaution, and the fast is valid.

Q: If a person knows that they will travel from their place of residence before the zenith, are they permitted to break their fast before they travel?

A: No, they are not permitted to do so. The person must refrain from fast-nullifiers until they leave and reach a point where they can no longer see the people at the border of their city of residence (*hadd al-tarrakhuss*).

Q: If one knows that something will occur, other than travel, that will excuse them from fasting, such as illness, menstruation, or post-partum bleeding, is it permissible to break the fast before its actual occurrence?

A: It is not permissible. One must refrain from all fast-nullifiers (e.g., eating) until the excuse's actual occurrence.

## One Who Will Not Experience Harm or Extreme Hardship Because of Old Age

If one has reached an old age (e.g., seventy or eighty), and it causes weakness and difficulty fasting, the ruling is that the person has the choice whether to fast or not.

- If they do not fast, they do not need to make up the fast.
- Penance: Yes (fidyah)

## Questions

Q: What if an elderly person becomes so weak that they are entirely unable to fast and are considered religiously excused? Are they required to fast?

A: They are permitted not to fast, and there is no need to make up the fasts nor pay a penance.

## One Who Is Not Suffering from Polydipsia

Polydipsia is an illness due to which a person feels extreme thirst, which occurs to the point that their thirst is not quenched.[23] The ruling for these individuals is that it is their choice whether they fast or not.

- If they do not fast, they do not need to make up the fast.
- Penance: Yes (fidyah)

---

23. Polydipsia is not just the feeling of thirst that any person might experience; it is a condition that has specific clinical symptoms.

Chapter 4

# How Do We Fast in the Month of Ramadan?

It is obligatory for one who wants to fast in the month of Ramadan to

- make an intention—one must intend to fast to seek nearness to Allah (swt); and
- refrain from all fast-nullifiers.

## Questions

Q: When must one make the intention to fast?

A: One may make the intention to fast the entire month either from

- its start;
- every night for the following day; or
- a little before the dawn of the day of fasting.

It is important that one has the intention to fast from dawn (fajr) to sunset.

Q: Does a person have to be mindful at every moment of their intention, or is it enough that it exists within oneself, even if it is in such a manner that they know they are fasting if asked, but do not think of it at every moment?

A: It is enough that the person is aware of it within themselves (*niyyah irtikaziyyah*).

Q: If it is dawn (fajr) and one is inattentive (*ghaflah*) or ignorant that one must make the intention, then becomes attentive before partaking of a fast-nullifier, do they still have time to make the intention and is their fast valid?

A: Yes, the fast is valid, except if the person became attentive to it after the zenith, in which case they must [continue] the fast but make it up later based on obligatory precaution.

Q: If a person makes the intention to fast, then after dawn they intend to break their fast or become hesitant, and then decide to fast before partaking of a fast-nullifier, is the fast valid?

A: They must complete their fast based on obligatory precaution but then make it up later.

Q: If someone does an act and is unsure if it breaks their fast, then the person asks and finds out that it does not break their fast, does the state of hesitation break the fast?

A: No

Q: Is the person intending to fast required to know the fast-nullifiers in detail?

A: No

Q: What types of things must the fasting person avoid during the day?

A: There are eight fast-nullifiers.

## The Eight Fast-Nullifiers to Avoid

These are the eight fast-nullifiers that break the fast and must be avoided during the daytime:
- Eating
- Drinking

- Intercourse
- Masturbating
- Vomiting
- Liquid enema
- Ascribing lies to Allah (swt) or His messenger (pbuh&hp) or the Imams (pbut)
- Allowing heavy dust or smoke into the throat

## First and second: Eating and drinking

Eating and drinking in large or small amounts breaks the fast. This includes even the small bits of food that remain between the teeth, whether it is normal food and drink such as bread or water or abnormal items such as debris (e.g., bitten nail, plastic, wood) or oil.

### QUESTIONS

Q: Is it permissible to swallow the saliva that accumulates in the mouth?

A: Yes

Q: Is it permissible to swallow what comes out of the lungs, such as sputum and the like?

A: Yes, it is permissible to swallow.

Q: There are eye and ear drops that, when administered, leave a taste in the mouth. Will they affect the validity of the fast?

A: No, it will not affect the validity of the fast.

Q: Will infused medicine or one poured over an open wound on the body, which eventually reaches the inside of the body, break the fast?

A: No, they will not affect the validity of the fast.

Q: Will medicine administered to the muscle (intramuscular) break the fast?

A: No, it will not break the fast.

Q: Does the previous ruling include intravenous (IV) administration?

A: Yes, although it is a recommended precaution to avoid it.

Q: Does the use of an inhaler, which is used by asthmatics, nullify the fast?

A: No, it does not nullify the fast if the inhaled medicine goes into the airway (breathing passageway) and not the esophagus (where the food and drink go).

Q: What about a pill that dissolves under the tongue and then enters the esophagus?

A: It breaks the fast. However, if the glands within the mouth absorb the medication, and it does not mix with the oral saliva such that it does not enter the esophagus, then it will not break the fast.

Q: What about something that reaches the throat through the nose?

A: It breaks the fast just like something that enters through the mouth.

## Third: Intercourse

QUESTIONS

Q: What is meant by intercourse (*juma*)?

A: It is the insertion of the head of the male penis into the female vagina even without seminal discharge (ejaculation).

## Fourth: Masturbation

Any act that provokes sexual arousal leading to male or female ejaculation, even if it is Islamically legal, such as sexual playfulness with one's spouse, breaks the fast.

QUESTIONS

Q: What if ejaculation occurs without actively causing it, such as passive ejaculation due to a wet dream?

A: It does not break the fast.

Q: What if one actively does something that sexually arouses, without intending ejaculation, yet they do ejaculate?

A: There are two scenarios here:

- One was confident that one would not ejaculate but then did.
    - It does not break the fast.
- One knew that it could cause ejaculation.
    - The fast is broken.
        - One must make up the fast.
        - Penance: Yes (kaffarah)

## Fifth: Vomiting

Intentional vomiting, even if it is a method of curing one's self of an illness such as food poisoning, breaks the fast. For example, if a person vomits to protect their own health, then the ruling is that the fast is broken, even though one does have permission to do so under such circumstances.

QUESTIONS

Q: What if the vomiting was not intentional?

A: The fast is still valid.

Q: What if food enters the mouth because of burping something from the throat?

A: It is not permissible to swallow that food. The fast is broken based on obligatory precaution if the person does so.

## Sixth: Liquid enema

Liquid enemas administered to the anus break the fast. However, solid enemas do not break the fast.

## Seventh: Ascribing lies to Allah, His messenger, or the infallible Imams

Ascribing lies to Allah (swt), His messenger (pbuh&hp), or one of the infallible Imams (pbut), irrespective of whether it is in the context of their general advice or a religious verdict, breaks the fast based on obligatory precaution.

## Questions

Q: What if one meant to say the truth but later found out that it was a lie?

A: The fast is still valid.

Q: What if one meant to lie but later found out that it was the truth?

A: The person must complete their fast based on obligatory precaution with the intention that this may be required by Allah (*raja al-matlubiyyah*).[24] However, they need to make up the fast.

Q: What if a person is fasting and wanted to state a saying from the Prophet (pbuh&hp) or the Imams (pbut) as reported by a particular source but is unsure if they truly said it?

A: The person may narrate it but must cite the source—for example, "in the book of *Al-kafi* by way of the Prophet (pbuh&hp)" or "by way of al-Sadiq (p)" rather than directly quoting the infallible.

Q: If one makes errors when reading the Holy Quran, is it permissible for one to read it and still ensure their fast is valid?

A: Yes, the fast is valid if the person does not intend to ascribe lies to the Holy Quran.

---

24. Raja al-matlubiyyah means "hope that it is required by Allah." It is an intention for an act of worship (e.g., fasting, prayer) that the jurist cannot establish with certainty that it is in fact legislated by God (i.e., *wajib*).

## Eighth: Allowing heavy dust or smoke to enter the throat

Allowing heavy dust or smoke to enter the throat breaks the fast.

Dust: There is no difference between the dust from flour, to which workers in flour mills are exposed, and other heavy dust.

Smoke: There is no difference between tobacco smoke and other smoke, such as that from machines and automobiles.

Note: It is considered to be a fast-nullifier based on obligatory precaution.

Q: Many women ask about the steam from pots and cookware that surrounds their noses and mouths when cooking. Should they avoid breathing in the steam?

A: The fast is valid, no matter how heavy the steam.

## Questions

Q: There are some things that some people think may be fast-nullifiers. Are the following fast-nullifiers?

- Sexual playfulness between spouses without intercourse or ejaculation and without intending either one
- Bleeding from a tooth extraction or something similar
- Using perfume—whether wearing it or smelling it

- Mascara on the eyes
- Dunking one's head or body into water

A: None of these break the fast, although some of them are abhorred while fasting—such as dunking one's head in water, which is highly abhorred, and its avoidance is a recommended precaution.

Q: What about brushing the teeth with toothpaste?

A: It is permissible with the condition that nothing remains in the mouth from the toothpaste such that none of it enters the esophagus.

**Special Notes Related to Janabah or Ghusl**

- Be aware that one must not remain in a state of janabah until dawn.
- The same applies to a woman who is no longer menstruating or having post-partum bleeding at night—it is obligatory for her to fast the next day. Therefore, she must perform major ablution (ghusl) before dawn.

Q: Must a woman in a state of greater *istihadha kubra* (non-menstrual bleeding) perform the ghusl at night and during the day to fast?

A: It is only obligatory for her prayers, like other days of the year.

Q: What is the ruling if a person was not aware of their state of janabah until dawn?

A: The fast is valid. The same rule applies if they were in a state of janabah and assumed that they did the ghusl only to later become aware that they did not.

Q: What is the ruling if a woman in menses (haydh) or post-partum bleeding (nifas) were to forget to do the ghusl until dawn?

A: Her fast is valid.

- If she remembers directly after dawn, her fast is valid and she only has to perform the ghusl before praying.
- If she remembers a day or more later, her fast is valid. However, she must make up the prayers (qada) that she made before performing the ghusl.

Q: If a person becomes in a state of janabah (mujnib) while awake or asleep and then becomes aware of their state (of janabah), is it permissible for the person to sleep before washing the ghusl of janabah?

A: Yes, it is permissible to do so, unless the person is sure that they will not wake up in time to do the ghusl of janabah before dawn.

Q: If one sleeps with the intention that they will do the ghusl of janabah before dawn, but they do not wake up, what should they do?

A: There are two cases here:

- If they were sure that they would wake up in time but did not, then they continue to fast, and the fast is valid.
- If they were unsure or doubtful [about being able to wake in time to perform ghusl, then they must fast that day, and they must make up the fast by obligatory precaution.

Q: What if the mujnib, or a woman in menses or post-partum bleeding, cannot perform the ghusl because of an illness or a lack of time or other excuses; is *tayammum* then enough?

A: Yes, it is enough in place of the ghusl. If the person was not to perform the tayammum, then the ruling would be the same as for the one who decided intentionally to remain in their state until dawn (fajr).

Q: If one does tayammum, is there a requirement to stay awake until dawn?

A: No, it is permissible for the person to sleep.

Q: If the person makes themselves mujnib in the last minutes of the night in which there is no time to do the ghusl before dawn, what is the ruling?

A: There are three cases here:

- The person does tayammum instead of ghusl.
    - The fast is valid.
    - They do not need to make up the fast.
- The person was inattentive of the time.
    - The fast is valid.
    - They do not need to make up the fast.
- If the person knew and did not perform the tayammum on purpose, then they have defied the obligatory precaution by doing so.
    - The fast is invalid.
    - They need to make up the fast.
    - Penance: Yes (kaffarah)

Q: If there was enough time for ghusl but the person decided to perform tayammum, what is the ruling?

A: There are two scenarios here:

- The person did tayammum with enough time for ghusl.
    - Tayammum is invalid, and the ghusl must be performed before prayer.
    - The person continues to fast.
    - They must make up the fast.
- The person was delayed until there was only enough time for tayammum.
    - Tayammum is valid, and the ghusl must be performed before prayer.
    - The fast is valid.

Q: If a person who is fasting has a nocturnal emission during the daytime in the month of Ramadan, must they hurry to do the ghusl?

A: No, it is permissible to delay the ghusl until the time of prayer. Furthermore, if the ghusl was not performed the entire day, the fast would still be valid.

Chapter 5

# When Does the Month of Ramadan Begin and End?

## The Beginning and Ending of the Lunar Month

The beginning of the month of Ramadan, like the other months, occurs when the moon moves out of its new moon phase into a waxing crescent and there is an appearance of the illuminated part of the moon (reflection of light from the sun on the edge of the moon) on the horizon at the sunset of the twenty-ninth or thirtieth day of the month of Shaban.

The end of the month is determined by the sighting of the crescent moon on the horizon again after the twenty-ninth or thirtieth day, and this will be the crescent moon of the month of Shawwal.

## Proving the Presence of the Crescent Moon on the Horizon

There are two ways of proving the presence of the crescent moon on the horizon:

- The passing of thirty days of the previous month (*itmam iddah*), because a lunar month has no more than thirty days. With the passing of thirty days, the month ends and the new month begins the following day.
- Sighting the crescent moon at sunset on the twenty-ninth day, marking the end of one month and the start of the next

## When Does the Month of Ramadan Begin and End?

The phrase "crescent moon sighting" refers to the sighting of the moon with the naked eye by the individual themselves and the sighting by others, so

- if a person sights the crescent moon themselves, then it is proven to that person that the start of the new month will be the next day, even if others did not see it—if the person is sure of the accuracy of their own sighting without the possibility of error; or
- if a person does not sight the crescent moon themselves, but it is proven to them that others have viewed it themselves, then it is enough for the person to determine the beginning of the next month to be the following day.[25]

## Questions

Q: How is the sighting of others proven?

A: It is proven by one of the following methods:

- The testimony of two just men that they have sighted the crescent themselves. However, their testimony is unacceptable in the following cases:
  - Knowledge of or knowing they are in error with contentment
  - A discrepancy in their testimonies through which one can determine that

---

25. The phrase "... others have viewed it themselves ..." means at least two just (*adil*) gentlemen who sighted the crescent by themselves.

they did not have the same sighting. For example, one states that they saw the convex end of the crescent closer to the earth while the other saw it to the left.
    - A testimony that contradicts theirs. For example, a group goes out to sight the moon and only two claim they saw it while the others did not, and the whole group had the same visual capacity and knowledge of where to look, with the assumption of optimal viewing conditions of clear skies and horizons.
- The testimony of many that they saw the crescent, such that it reaches the level of *tawatur* or widespread news from which one can attain knowledge or contentment.
- It is proven to the religious jurist of emulation (*marja*), such that one feels certain and content that the crescent moon was sighted or in the testimony of the two just witnesses with the preceding stipulations.

Q: If more than one person witnesses the crescent moon but the detailed scientific predictions ensure that the moon is still in its new moon phase, or the astronomical observatories forecast the difficulty of sighting it using their telescopes, does this prevent us from taking the testimonies of the witnesses?

A: Normally, in such a situation, certainty is not attained that the crescent moon exists in a state that makes it visible. Therefore, the testimonies are unacceptable.

Q: If there were two just witnesses among those who sighted the crescent moon, what is the ruling?

A: One may depend upon the evidence [those two just witnesses provided], if there is no knowledge of their being in error with contentment (as previously explained).

Q: Is it enough to prove the sighting of the crescent moon that accurate astronomical calculations determine the waxing crescent and that there is contentment in their accuracy?

A: It is not enough, unless there is contentment that it in fact appears on the horizons in a manner that makes it visible for sighting.

Q: If one cannot view the crescent moon with the naked eye, is it enough for one to use a telescope to prove the crescent moon?

A: No, it is not enough.

Q: If the crescent moon cannot be seen in one's own city (or area of land), is it enough for one to depend on the sighting in another city?

A: It is not enough, unless the sighting in the other city dictates that it would also be seen in the person's own city if it were not for barriers such as clouds, dust, mountains, or the like.

Q: When does the sighting in one city (or area of land) dictate the sighting in another?

A: In two cases:

- When both cities share the same horizons of sunset and sunrise, with one being north or south of the other
- When the city where the sighting occurred is east of the person's own city and there is only a minor difference in their lines of latitude

Q: What if the city from which the crescent moon is sighted is west of the person's own city, such as if the crescent is sighted in Damascus and the person is in Baghdad?

A: The sighting is insufficient to prove the beginning of the month in the person's city. However, if the crescent moon remains in the sky in the city where it was viewed for a period of time that is longer than the normal difference in time between the sunrise and sunset between both cities, this will reveal that there is a probability of sighting the crescent moon in the person's own city, even if it is not actually seen.[26]

Q: Is it possible to determine from the following characteristics of the crescent moon, when it is sighted during the sunset of the twenty-ninth day, that it is two days old?
- Its high altitude on the horizon
- The aura around the moon
- Its remaining on the horizon for an hour or more

---

26. For example, if the sunset in Detroit was at 7:00 p.m. and in Chicago it was at 7:45 p.m., and the crescent moon was visible in Chicago for fifty-five minutes, then this reveals that there is a probability of sighting the crescent moon in Detroit. But, if the crescent moon remains visible on the horizon in Chicago for a time that is approximately less than forty-five minutes, then there is no probability of the sighting in Detroit.

A: No, the most that these cases signify is that a long time before the sunset, the moon moved out of its new moon phase into the waxing crescent phase. It does not prove that it could have been sighted at the sunset of the previous night.

Q: If it is the night of the twenty-ninth day (the eve of the thirtieth day) of the month of Shaban, and the crescent moon is not sighted, is it permissible to fast the following day (the thirtieth of Shaban)?

A: It is permissible to fast that day; however, one's intention must be for the last day of Shaban (recommended fast), except if an obligatory make-up fast from a previous month of Ramadan is owed—then the intention must be to make up that missed fast.

Q: Using the same scenario from the previous question, what if one were to fast that day (the thirtieth day of Shaban) and it then became apparent that it was the first day of the month of Ramadan?

A: The fast is valid and is considered to be for the first day of the month of Ramadan.

Q: If it is the night of the twenty-ninth day of the month of Ramadan and the crescent moon was not sighted, is it obligatory for one to fast the next day (the thirtieth day)?

A: Yes, unless it becomes apparent to the person during the daytime that it is indeed the first day of the month of Shawwal, in which case they must break their fast immediately.

Q: If the person were to fast that day only to find out at night that it was the first of Shawwal, will they have sinned by fasting on the Day of Eid?

A: No, because the person fasted without knowledge that it was the first day of Shawwal (the Day of Eid).

Chapter 6

# Rulings about Disrupting the Fast in the Month of Ramadan

## Fast Disruption Type 1

If a person disrupts their intention to fast during the daytime in the month of Ramadan, such that they did not make the intention to fast at all, delayed their intention past its allotted time, or broke their fast because of duplicity,[27] then the ruling is that the fast is invalid (even though none of the eight fast-nullifiers occurred), and one must make up the fast.

## Fast Disruption Type 2

If a person partakes of one of the fast-nullifiers on purpose, or stays in a state of janabah on purpose until dawn and was not forced or compelled to do so, the ruling is that they will have sinned and must refrain from eating [and from the rest of the fast-nullifiers] until maghrib. They must make up the fast and, in some cases [as will be mentioned in next few pages], they must pay kaffarah.

### Questions

Q: What if someone partakes of a fast-nullifier but not on purpose or not by choice (meaning by compulsion)?

A: The fast is valid, and in some cases (as in the following instances) nothing further is expected of the person.

---

27. Duplicity in making an intention to fast means the intention is made as a show for others with no full loyalty to Allah. [Editor]

*Rulings about Disrupting the Fast in the Month of Ramadan*

### ONE FORGETS ONE IS FASTING

If a person partakes of one of the fast-nullifiers because they forgot that they were fasting, the fast is valid.

For example, if one ate, drank, or had intercourse because they forgot they were fasting, or one stayed in a state of janabah until dawn, forgetful of fasting the next day, the fast is valid in both cases.

### ONE IS IGNORANT AND EATS, DRINKS, OR HAS INTERCOURSE

If a person eats, drinks, or has intercourse out of ignorance, the fast is broken. One must make up the fast, but there is no penance.

Examples:

- One ate something that is abnormal or drank medication with contentment that it was not a fast-nullifier thinking that only normally eaten foods break the fast, except for medicine.
- The person was content in the maghrib time and in the fact that there was no eastern redness in the sky. As a result, they ate or drank and then discovered that the sun had not set yet. However, if the reason for their belief was darkness (e.g., from heavy clouds) or the like, then the make-up fast is by obligatory precaution.
- One had doubt that it was dawn and decided that it was not dawn without checking and continued to eat. Then it became clear that it was dawn.

- However, if the person themselves actively checked whether it was dawn, determined that it was not, then ate or drank, and, after doing so, it became clear to the person that it was indeed dawn, then the fast is not broken.
- In neither case is there legally-binding (by Islamic law) evidence of dawn. Otherwise, they would have to make up the fast and pay kaffarah.

### ONE IS IGNORANT AND COMMITS ONE OF THE OTHER FAST-NULLIFIERS

If one partakes of a fast-nullifier other than eating, drinking, or intercourse or remains mujnib until dawn, ignorant that such acts must be avoided, the fast is

- valid if the ignorance is excused; or
- broken if the ignorance is inexcusable.

Example:

One is raised far from a religious environment and believes with certainty that masturbation does not break the fast, or one depends upon a proof that smoke does not break the fast, such as a religious verdict (*fatwa*) from a jurist of emulation (marja), and then it becomes clear that it is wrong to stay mujnib, it is not obligatory to make up the fast as long as one was ignorant and certain that it would not break the fast, whether there was an excuse or not.

*Rulings about Disrupting the Fast in the Month of Ramadan*

### ONE UNINTENTIONALLY PARTAKES OF ONE OF THE FAST-NULLIFIERS

If one unintentionally partakes of one of the fast-nullifiers, the fast is valid.

Examples:

- If someone is held down by force and water is poured down their throat, their fast is valid.
- If one is gargling for *wudu* or to clean their mouth, and water enters the throat unintentionally, the fast is valid.

There are two exceptions to this ruling:

- If one gargles with water to reduce their thirst and water unintentionally enters their throat, they must make up the fast.
- If someone began sexual playfulness with their spouse without the intention of ejaculation or intercourse and was unsure whether they would ejaculate or not and unintentionally does, they must make up the fast.

### ONE IS FORCED TO PARTAKE OF A FAST-NULLIFIER

If an oppressor forces someone to partake of a fast-nullifier using physical compulsion or fear of compulsion and they do so fearing harm, [there are slightly different rulings depending on the type of fast-nullifier].

- If the fast-nullifiers were eating, drinking, or intercourse, the fast is invalid.
    - One must make up the fast.
    - Penance: No

- If the fast-nullifiers were other fast-nullifiers, the fast is invalid by obligatory precaution.
    - One must make up the fast by obligatory precaution.
    - Penance: No

### STAYING MUJNIB UNTIL DAWN

If one stays mujnib until dawn because they are unable to do ghusl or tayammum due to lack of water or sand or out of fear of an oppressor, the fast is valid and they do not need to make up the fast.

### FURTHER CLARIFICATION

A person who breaks their fast by partaking of one of the fast-nullifiers must abstain from any more fast-nullifiers until maghrib, and it is sufficient for them to make the intention that they are fasting to fulfill that which Allah actually requires of them (whether it is to actually fast or to abstain).

## Fast Disruption Type 3

A make-up fast and kaffarah are both obligatory for someone who breaks their fast with the first four fast-nullifiers (eating, drinking, intercourse, or masturbation) if they fulfill the following criteria:

- Committing the fast-nullifier is intentional. The following are some exceptions where a make-up fast is required without kaffarah [because there was absence of intention]:
    - One gargles to reduce thirst, and water enters the esophagus unintentionally.

## Rulings about Disrupting the Fast in the Month of Ramadan

- One partakes of an act that arouses them, causing ejaculation unintentionally, even if they were unsure that they would ejaculate. However, if the act that aroused them sexually was a kiss, touching or foreplay, then they must pay the kaffarah.
- Committing the fast-nullifier is without compulsion. For example, if an oppressor threatens a person to break their fast, and they break it out of fear of those threats, they must make up the fast, but there is no penance.
- Not being confident that partaking of the act would break their fast. If, however, one was sure that it was permissible, then there is no kaffarah, whether because they thought fasting was not obligatory for them (e.g., because they were too young) or because they thought it was not a fast-nullifier at all. The kaffarah is not obligatory for an ignorant person who is sure that it is permissible to partake of a fast-nullifier, whether their ignorance is excused or unexcused.
  - An example of unexcused ignorance is a person who is *muqassir* (did not make the necessary effort to learn the laws), and this led to their believing something that is not true.

## Questions

Q: If someone partakes of one of the first four fast-nullifiers knowing that it will break their fast, but they do not know that such an act requires kaffarah, must the person still pay the kaffarah?

A: Yes. Ignorance of the kaffarah is not a valid excuse for not paying it.

Q: What if someone were to partake of one of the other four fast-nullifiers (vomiting; liquid enema; ascribing lies to Allah [swt], His messenger [pbuh&hp], or the Imams [pbut]; or breathing in heavy smoke or dust); are they required to pay the kaffarah?

A: No. However, they will have committed a sin if done intentionally and without compulsion.

Q: What if one stays mujnib until dawn?

A: One must pay it if it is intentional and without compulsion.

Q: A person breaks their fast thinking that it is maghrib without certainty that it is. If this person were to find out later that they had broken their fast before maghrib, must they pay the kaffarah?

A: The person must pay the kaffarah whether they find out that they broke their fast early or not. The reason for the kaffarah in both cases is that the person acted without legitimate purpose. They should have been certain.

Q: What is the kaffarah for intentionally breaking one's fast in the month of Ramadan?

A: For each day missed, it is enough to either

- fast two consecutive months; or
- feed sixty impoverished people (one *mudd* [1.65 lb.] of food per person).

It is enough for the kaffarah to be either through

- giving cooked food that satisfies a person's hunger; or
- giving one mudd (1.65 lb.) of wheat or any type of appropriate equivalent food.

It is not acceptable to pay the cost of the food to the person in need.

## Fast Disruption Type 4

For those for whom fasting in the month of Ramadan is an obligation and they either did not fast or their fast was invalid (with an excuse or without one), it is obligatory to make up the fast of each day missed after the month of Ramadan ends.

As for those not required to fast in the month of Ramadan because they did not fulfill one of its conditions, they do not have to make up the fasts. However, people with the following conditions **are** required to make up the fasts.

- One who is harmed by fasting. Once the harm no longer exists, one must make up the fasts.
    - If the harm was to one's health and the situation continues until the following Ramadan, one does not need to make up the fasts, but one must pay fidyah for each day of missed fast.
- A woman in a state of menses or post-partum bleeding must make up the fasts.
- If one did not fast due to difficult or unusual conditions such that reasonable people deem

it normally unbearable, they must make up the fasts if they are able.
- One who was legally traveling must make up the fasts.

## Questions

Q: Must one hasten to make up the fasts of the month of Ramadan or may they be delayed for a year or more?

A: One may delay the make-up fasts if the delay is not so long that they become heedless of their responsibility to Allah. If one completes the make-up fasts before the next Ramadan, there is no penance. However, if they delay making up the fasts until after the next Ramadan, they must pay fidyah for each day of fast missed and made up.

Q: Is it obligatory for one to make up the fasts on consecutive days?

A: It is not obligatory. A person who owes two make-up fasts may do a make-up fast for the first day in one month and for the second in another month.

Q: Is it obligatory for one to make up the fasts in the order that they were missed?

A: It is not obligatory—it is each individual's choice which they make up first.

Q: How must one make up the fast?

A: The make-up fast is no different than the regular fast except in the intention. The intention may be made in two ways:

- One makes an intention of a make-up fast (qada) in place of the missed fast. The intention will not suffice without including "in place of the missed fast."
- If one has not partaken of a fast-nullifier, they still can make the intention before the zenith, after which it is by obligatory precaution that they may not make the intention.

Q: If a person had intended another fast other than the make-up fast (sawm qada), then wanted to change their intention to the make-up fast before the zenith, are they allowed?

A: No

Q: If someone's intention is the make-up fast, must they continue their fast to maghrib or can they break their fast during the daytime and then fast another day instead?

A: There are two cases here:

- If the fast is broken before the zenith, then yes.
- If they hope to break the fast after the zenith, then no.
    - If someone wanted to intentionally break their make-up fast after the zenith, they would have to make up the make-up fast and pay kaffarah of feeding ten impoverished people one mudd (1.65 lb.) each. If they are unable to pay kaffarah, they must fast three days.

Q: If one knows that they owe make-up fasts but are unsure of the number, what should they do?

A: It is enough to make up the amount that they are certain they missed.

Q: What about one who knows that they owe one or more days of fasts of Ramadan and then has doubt if they made them up or not?

A: It is obligatory for the person to make them up so that they can be certain that they fulfilled their obligations.

# In Closing

At the beginning and at the end of all endeavors, all thanks and praise are to Allah (swt) and may the peace and blessings of Allah be upon Prophet Muhammad and his purified progeny.

# Appendix

## Important Documents about Horizon and Astronomical Data

This appendix consists of several edicts and directions either from His Eminence Grand Ayatullah Sayyid al-Sistani or his office in the Holy City of Najaf during recent years. We saw fit to include these edicts because they are in line with the goal behind publishing this book of Islamic laws.

*Appendix*

# Document 1:
# Questions and Answers regarding the First Day of Shawwal 1428 AH

## *The question*

In the name of Allah, the Beneficent, the Merciful

All praises are to Allah, the Lord of the Worlds, and may His peace and blessings be bestowed upon His messenger Muhammad and his immaculate progeny.

The office of His Eminence Grand Ayatullah Sayyid Ali al-Sistani

Assalamu alaykum wa rahmatullahi wa barakatuh

RE: The crescent moons of the months of Ramadan and Shawwal for the year 1428

In an effort to avoid any unease or lack of clarity from which the Muslim community suffers in North America in identifying the eve of the first of the months of Ramadan and Shawwal, we mention (below) some information and conclusions surrounding this issue—noting that the conclusions are based on contentment resulting from astronomical calculations that are considered to be sufficient to determine the likelihood of the sighting of the crescent moon and, as such, aid in the determination of the first day of the months. We ask Your Eminence to confirm those conclusions that are correct and to amend those that are wrong, and we thank you.

First: The crescent moon of the blessed month of Ramadan will be born at 12:44 GMT on Tuesday, September 11, 2007, and cannot be seen with the naked eye on the eve

## Appendix

of Wednesday anywhere in the world. However, sighting this crescent moon with the naked eye is possible in certain parts of North America on the eve of Thursday, September 13, 2007.

Second: The crescent moon of the month of Shawwal will be born at 5:00 GMT on Thursday, October 11, 2007. The sighting of the crescent moon, with the naked eye, will be possible on the west coast of South America on the eve of Friday, October 12, 2007—noting that that coast is considered to be to the east of North America. The sighting will also be possible in the Polynesian islands that are to the west of the aforementioned coast that has a unity of the night with North America.

Third: Based on the above, for the followers of the *maraje* who have the juristic opinion of the unity of the horizons, the first of the month of Ramadan will be Thursday, September 13, 2007, as well as for those who have continued to emulate a deceased marja who has the juristic opinion of the unity of horizons and in contemporary issues they follow a grand jurist who does not adopt the same opinion. For these two groups, the first of the month of Shawwal will be Friday, October 12, 2007.

Fourth: As for those who follow those grand jurists who do not have the opinion of the unity of the horizons, the first of the holy month of Ramadan will be Thursday, September 13, 2007, in the area in which the sighting will be possible. As for other areas, the first of the holy month of Ramadan will be Friday, September 14, 2007. Therefore, for this group, the first of the month of

Shawwal will be Saturday, October 13, 2007, if they are residing in North America.

NOTES:

- The times of the crescent moon birth and the ability to sight it are taken from www.moonsighting.com.
- North America is special with respect to its geography in that the difference in time between it and Iraq or the Gulf nations can reach or exceed twelve hours, which means that the crescent moon sighting can occur there a night before it is seen in Iraq and the Gulf countries.

With this we ask Allah, the Almighty, that He reward you, on our behalf and on behalf of all Muslims, the reward of the good-doers.

Assalamu alaykum wa rahmatullahi wa barakatuh

A group of those residing in North America

## The answer

What was mentioned is correct with the attainment of contentment in the ability to see [the crescent moon] if it were not for the clouds and similar obstructions.

The seal of the office of Sayyid al-Sistani
The Holy City of Najaf
12/11/1428

# Appendix

## Copy of the original document

بسم الله الرحمن الرحيم

والحمد لله رب العالمين ، والصلاة والسلام على سيد الخلق محمد وأهل بيته الطيبين الطاهرين.

مكتب سماحة آية الله السيد علي السيستاني دام ظله

السلام عليكم ورحمة الله وبركاته

الموضوع: هلال شهري رمضان وشوال لسنة ١٤٢٨

تفادياً للإرباك وعدم الوضوح الذي تعاني منه عادة الجالية الإسلامية في أمريكا الشمالية عند تحديد ليلتي الأول من شهري رمضان وشوال ، نذكر أدناه بعض المعلومات والإستنتاجات ذات العلاقة بهذا الموضوع. علماً بأن الإستنتاجات قد بنيت على فرض أن الإطمئنان الناتج من الحسابات الفلكية يكفي لثبوت بداية الشهر. ونرجو من سماحتكم تأكيد الصحيح من تلك الإستنتاجات وتصحيح الخطأ منها وشكراً.

أولاً: يولد هلال شهر رمضان المبارك في الساعة ١٢:٤٤ بتوقيت جرينيش يوم الثلاثاء ١١ أيلول ٢٠٠٧. رؤية هذا الهلال بالعين المجردة غير ممكنة ليلة الأربعاء في أي مكان في العالم. ولكن روؤية هذا الهلال بالعين المجردة تكون ممكنة في أجزاء من أمريكا الشمالية ليلة الخميس ١٣ أيلول ٢٠٠٧.

ثانياً: يولد هلال شهر شوال في الساعة ٥:٠٠ بتوقيت جرينيش يوم الخميس ١١ تشرين الأول ٢٠٠٧. روؤية هذا الهلال بالعين المجردة تكون ممكنة في الساحل الجنوبي الغربي من أمريكا الجنوبية ليلة الجمعة ١٢ تشرين الأول ٢٠٠٧ ، علماً بان هذا الساحل يعتبر شرق أمريكا الشمالية. وهذه الرؤية تكون أيضاً ممكنة في جزر تسمى الجزر البوليزية والتي تقع غرب الساحل المذكور ولها ليل مشترك مع أمريكا الشمالية.

ثالثاً: بناءً على ماتقدم ، يكون الأول من شهر رمضان المبارك يوم الخميس ١٣ أيلول ٢٠٠٧ بالنسبة لمقلدي المراجع الذين يقولون بوحدة الأفق ، وكذلك من إستمر على تقليد من يقول بوحدة الأفق بعد وفاته ويقلد في المستجدات من لا يقول بوحدة الأفق. و يكون الأول من شهر شوال لهؤلاء يوم الجمعة ١٢ تشرين الأول ٢٠٠٧.

# Appendix

رابعاً: أما بالنسبة لمقلدي المراجع الذين لايقولون بوحدة الأفــق: يكون الأول من شهر رمضان المبارك يوم الخميس ١٣ أيلول ٢٠٠٧ في المناطق التي تكون فيها الرؤية ممكنة وماعدا ذلك يكون الأول من شهر رمضان المبارك يوم الجمعة ١٤ أيلول ٢٠٠٧. و يكون الأول من شهر شــوال لــهؤلاء يوم الـسبت ١٣ تشــرين الأول ٢٠٠٧ إن كان مقيماً في أمريكا الشمالية.

( ملاحظة ١: مواعيد ولادة الــهلال وإمكانيــة الرؤية مأخوذة من موقع على الشبكة العالمية للمعلومات إسمه:
( www.moonsighting.com )

(ملاحظة ٢: أمريكا الشمالية لها خصوصية من ناحية الموقع الجغرافي حيث إن فرق التوقيت مع العراق ودول الخليج قد يصل أو يتعدى ال ١٢ ساعة، مما يتسبب في إمكانية ثبوت الهلال فيها ليلة قبل ثبوته في العراق ودول الخليج)

هذا ونبتهل الى الباري جل وعلا أن يجزيكم عنا وعن جميع المسلمين خير جزاء المحسنين.

والسلام عليكم ورحمة الله وبركاته

مجموعة من المقيمين في أمريكا الشمالية

*Appendix*

# Document 2: The Horizon in the School of al-Sayyid al-Sistani

## *Introduction*

The office of His Eminence, the Supreme Jurist of Emulation, Sayyid al-Sistani (may Allah prolong his life)

Assalamu alaykum wa rahmatullah, and our prayers are for your prolonged life and continued health.

A group of believers in North America would like to inquire about something that was mentioned in *Minhaj al-salihin* and other sources that "the unity of the horizons" only occurs for two lands if the sighting in the first land is associated with the sighting of the crescent in the second land, even if it was not sighted because of dust or clouds.

Based on the figure below, both because of contentment and experience, the areas that are in orange or dark yellow are the areas in which the crescent moon can be seen with the naked eye under ideal conditions—such as clear skies. However, in the other areas, the age of the crescent moon would be more than forty hours after its birth (as an example) and contentment in the ability to sight the crescent is attained based on astronomical data, such as the red area on the map that depicts the areas in which the sighting was proven through tawatur (those who sighted the crescent gave the same description of the crescent, and such diverse groups could not possibly conspire to lie about the matter), and through repeated experiences that there surely is an ability to sight the crescent in this area with ease and clarity.

## The question

Based upon the criteria mentioned in *Minhaj al-salihin* and based on scientific proof as well as the practical experience of the ability to sight the crescent in the red region, may we interpret the phrase in *Minhaj* of "the unity of horizons" to include all of the areas that are within the red region without paying attention to the areas next to the dark yellow region in which there is neither contentment nor a great probability of sighting the crescent moon? Therefore, as an example, may we say that if the crescent sighting has been proven religiously in the city of Los Angeles, then it will also be sighted in the city of Miami and in Ecuador as a result of the association [or relationship] between the areas in the sighting—based on experience and contentment in the astronomical data?

Please benefit us with your response, may Allah (swt) reward you.

## The answer

If it is proven surely that the crescent moon in the areas that fall close to the edge of the red region are at an altitude and size close to those of the crescent in the areas after it, in which the crescent moon was indeed sighted with clarity, then contentment is usually attained that such a relationship between the two areas exists. This is contrary to the case in which it may be expected that the crescent in those areas is smaller in size or lower in altitude to the extent that it is not possible to

## Appendix

sight the crescent moon with the naked eye, even if the astronomers made the claim that it is indeed possible.

The seal of the office of Ayatullah Sayyid Ali al-Sistani
The Holy City of Najaf
Rajab 8, 1429

# Appendix

## Copy of the original document

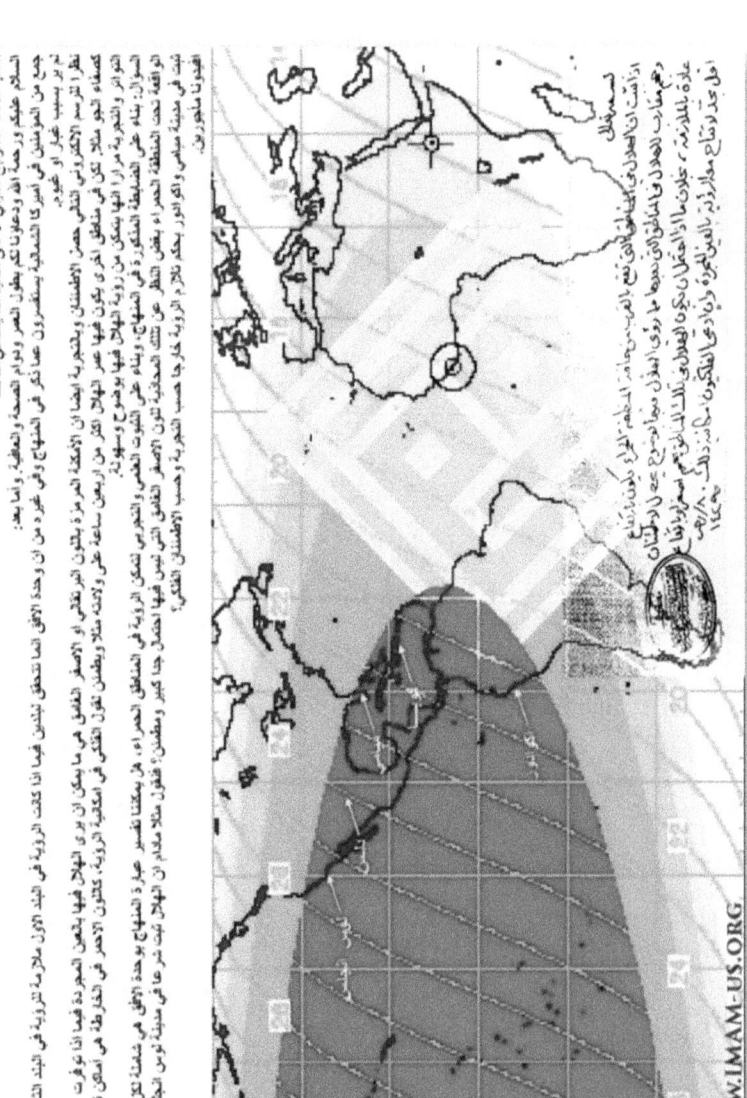

Appendix

# Document 3:
# The Horizon Criteria and Advice

## *The question*

An edict with the stamp of His Eminence Ayatullah al-Sistani (may Allah prolong his life) in which he explains the conditions for the sighting of the crescent and the most important principles that are criteria in determining "the unity of the horizons," along with his directions in resolving the differences between the believers that result from differences in the verdicts of their jurists of emulation

In the name of Allah, the Beneficent, the Merciful

To His Eminence, the Supreme Jurist of the Sect, Grand Ayatullah Sayyid al-Sistani (may Allah prolong his esteemed life)

Assalamu alaykum wa rahmatullahi wa barakatuh.

We would like to keep Your Eminence apprised of a monthly meeting held by six scholars who are responsible for Islamic centers of the followers of the school of Ahl al-Bayt (pbut) in London to discuss issues of importance to the sect. In their last session, these scholars discussed the issue of the crescent in Britain, and they noticed that there is general dismay and great unrest as a result of the differences between the jurists on the criteria for the sighting of the crescent moon, especially when the difference occurs in determining the first of the month or three days for Eid, as was the

## Appendix

case last year, which created unrest that was difficult to resolve.

As a result of this gathering, we would like to present you with a summary of the issues discussed:

- Based on the astronomical criteria and the testimony of those of expertise, the crescent moon can be sighted in most of Europe before sunset next Friday using a telescope (a visual aid).

If the criteria for sighting the crescent moon, according to your esteemed insight, is "the scientific and astronomical association" between sighting the crescent moon in one land and sighting it in another land if it were not for obstructions, then may this association be generalized to include the lines of longitude also, or is this relationship specific to the lines of latitude only?

We hope that Your Eminence will help us in making the correct decision that decreases the differences between families in Europe and the United Kingdom especially. We ask that you remain a refuge and support to the nation by Muhammad and his immaculate progeny [we ask Allah].

### The answer

In the name of the Almighty

- The chosen criterion for ascertaining the beginning of the lunar month in every land is the appearance of the crescent moon on the horizons of that land, in a manner that it can be seen with the naked eye if it were not for (atmospheric) obstructions such as clouds, fog, or the like. Based on this criterion, the ability to see with an optical aid (telescope) alone is insufficient.

The unity of the horizons between two lands in the sighting of the crescent moon means that the actual sighting in the first land is associated with the sighting in the second land if it were not for external (atmospheric) obstructions. As it is well-known, the most important matter that affects the sighting is how high (the altitude) the crescent moon is off the horizon at sunset. If the two lands share the same lines of latitude, that does not ensure the appearance of the crescent moon in both lands in the same night and with the same altitude. In addition, it is seen that, in many cases, the crescent moon can be sighted in most lands that lie to the south of the equator because it appears there at a suitable altitude, and it cannot be seen in the same night in many lands that fall in the Northern hemisphere of the earth—even if they share the same lines of longitude with the first land. That is because it (the moon) sets in those lands before sunset, or the crescent moon does not appear because it does not appear at a suitable altitude [to be sighted] above the horizons after sunset.

As a result of the differences between the jurists in the criteria for the start of the lunar month, the differences in the beginning of the lunar months usually cannot be avoided, and it is up to every individual to follow the verdict of their jurist of emulation (marja) as is the case with all Islamic laws in which jurists differ. It is

## Appendix

important that the believers are taught to accept the differences without making it an issue of contention and disgruntlement.

May Allah grant you success and support you in your steps.

Assalamu alaykum wa rahmatullahi wa barakatuh.

Signed and sealed: Ali al-Husseini al-Sistani
Shaban 26, 1430

# Appendix

## Copy of the original document

بسم الله الرحمن الرحيم

سماحة المرجع الديني الأعلى للطائفة آية الله العظمى السيد السيستاني دام ظله الوارف

السلام عليكم ورحمة الله وبركاته:-

نحيط مقامكم السامي علماً بأن اجتماعاً شهرياً ينعقد بحضور سنة من العلماء المسؤولين عن المراكز الإسلامية لاتباع مدرسة أهل البيت عليهم السلام في لندن، للتداول بشأن القضايا التي تهم الطائفة. ولقد ناقش العلماء المذكورون مسألة رؤية الهلال في بريطانيا في جلستهم الأخيرة، ولاحظوا أن هناك استياءً عاماً وضجة كبيرة ناتجة من اختلاف الفقهاء في صبيحة رؤية الهلال، خصوصاً أن الاختلاف في أول الشهر أو في العيد لثلاثة أيام كما حصل في العام الماضي أوجد إرباكاً تصعب الإجابة عليه.

وبهذه المناسبة نعرض إلى سماحتكم خلاصة ما تم بحثه:-

١- حسب الضوابط الفلكية وشهادة أهل الخبرة، فالإمكان رؤية الهلال في معظم أوربا قبل غروب الشمس يوم الجمعة القادم بالعين المسلحة.

٢- إذا كان الملاك في رؤية الهلال حسب نظركم الشريف هو (التلازم العلمي والفلكي) بين رؤية الهلال في بلد ورؤيته في بلد آخر لولا المانع، فهل بالإمكان تعميم التلازم على خطوط الطول أيضاً أو أنه يخص خطوط العرض فقط.

نرجو من سماحتكم مساعدتنا في اتخاذ القرار الصائب الذي يقلل الخلاف بين الأسر في أوربا والمملكة المتحدة على وجه الخصوص. ودمتم ملاذاً وسنداً للأمة محمد وآله الطاهرين.

بسم تعالى

١- المعتار أن المناط في دخول الشهر العربي في كل بلد هو دخوله الهلال في أفقه ذلك البلد بحيث يكون قابلاً للرؤية فيه المجردة لولا المانع من سحاب او غيرها مع ملاحظة مذهبي الإمكانية الرؤية للدين المسلح منها

٢- المستزاد في الأمين من بلدين في رؤية الهلال يعني أن تكون الرؤية الفعلية في البلد الأول ملازمة للرؤية في البلد الآخر لولا المانع الخارجي ومن المعلوم أن من أهم الأمور المؤثرة في الرؤية هو مدى ارتفاع الهلال عن الأفق عند الغروب ، ولبيد أن يتخلط الطول لا تفصح ظهور الهلال فيها في بلد واحد، للملاحظة أن في بعض الحالات يكون الهلال نازلاً للرؤية في معظم البلدان التي تقع في صوب ضبط الاستواء لطهوره فيها بارتفاع مناسب ، ولا يكن ربب في الليالي نفسها في أكثر من البلدان التي تقع في شمال الكرة الأرضية ۔ وإن كانت مشتركة مع البلدان الأولى في خطوط الطول ۔ وذلك لمزيد فيها قبل غروب الشمس أو عدم ظهوره فيها بارتفاع المناسب فوق الأفق لعدم الغروب

٣- إن الاختلاف في بداية الشهر العربي أو انقضاءه مسألة اجتهادية في ضوء اختلاف الفقهاء تبعاً لاختلاف الأخذ في دخول الشهر العربي وعليكم سعياً أن يبذل ذووكم وحرصهم في التقليد كما هو الحال في سائر المسائل الفقهية التي يختلف فيها الفقهاء ، وبسعي تبنف المؤمنين على تحمل الاختلاف في ذلك ، وعدم جعله مثاراً للنزاع والشاح.

ويفقكم الله ، وسدد خطاكم ، والسلام عليكم ورحمة الله وبركاته

٢٦ رجب ١٤٢٢

*Appendix*

# Document 4:
# A Practical Example

A release issued by the office of His Eminence Grand Ayatullah Sayyid al-Sistani (may Allah prolong his life) in the Holy City of Najaf regarding the announcement that the beginning of the month of Ramadan has been proven in the Holy City of Najaf and several countries in Europe and North America.

In this release is a clear proof of the principle of "the unity of the horizons" which is the [juristic] opinion of His Eminence Sayyid al-Sistani (may Allah prolong his life) and his definition of the lands and locations, even if sunset has not taken place in such lands yet.

The document states:
 In the name of Allah, the Beneficent, the Merciful

The office of His Eminence Sayyid al-Sistani in the Holy City of Najaf announces to the gracious believers that it has been proven to His Eminence (may Allah prolong his life) that tomorrow, Thursday, is the first day of the blessed month of Ramadan in most Islamic countries such as Iraq, the remaining Arab countries, Iran, Pakistan, Indonesia, Malaysia, as well as India, Australia, the African nations, the nations of South America, the United States, and areas of southern Canada. As for most regions of Europe such as Britain, Ireland, France, Germany, Italy, Belgium, Holland, the Scandinavian nations, and most regions of Canada, the first day of the holy month will be the day after tomorrow, Friday. We

*Appendix*

ask Allah Almighty to make it a month of goodness and blessings for all Muslims.

The seal of the office of Sayyid al-Sistani
The Holy City of Najaf
The eve of Thursday, Ramadan 1, 1431

## Appendix

## Copy of the original document

بسم الله الرحمن الرحيم

يعلن مكتب سماحة السيد السيستاني في النجف الاشرف المؤمنين الكرام انه تدنَّست لديه مساحته ثبوت هلال شهر رمضان (المبارك في معظم الدول الاسلامية كالعراق وسائر الدول العربية وايران وباكستان واندونيسيا وماليزيا وكذلك في الهند واستراليا و الدول الامريكية ودول امريكا الجنوبية والولايات المتحدة واجزاء من جنوب كندا . واما في اغلب مناطق اوروبا كبريطانيا وايرلندا وفرنسا والمانيا و ايطاليا وبلجيكا وهولندا والدول الاسكندنافية ومعظم اجزاء كندا فان يوم غد بعد غدٍ (الجمعة) سيكون اول ايام الشهر الفضيل . نسأل الله تبارك وتعالى ان يجعله شهر خير وبركة لجميع المسلمين.

ليلة الخميس ۸ رمضان
۱٤۳۱هـ

مكتب السيد السيستاني

# Glossary

***ahd*** (عَهْد). A promise or covenant that one makes with Allah that must be in the following form to be valid: "*Ahadtu Allaha* that I do such-and-such."

***baligh*** (بالغ). Reaching the time of bulugh.

***bulugh*** (بُلُوغ). The age at which a person becomes responsible for performing religious duties such as daily obligatory prayer and fasting during the month of Ramadan. A girl becomes *baligha* (reaches this time) upon completing nine lunar years, and a boy becomes baligh (reaches this time) upon completing fifteen lunar years except for when one of the signs of bulugh, such as the growth of stiff pubic hair or the discharge of semen, appears before that age.

***confirmed harm*** (ضَرَرٌ مُؤَكَّد). A harm that came about due to an actual situation as opposed to an opinion that it might happen.

***dhuhr*** (ظُهْر). Zenith.

***ejaculation*** (اسْتِمْناء). Usually referring to the seminal discharge from the male reproductive organ. In the case that one is unable to determine whether the discharge is semen or not, the following characteristics should be used:
- Release with arousal
- Gushing discharge
- Total physical relaxation (*futur*-فُتُور) after the complete release of the fluid

If such characteristics are fulfilled, then the fluid discharge is semen (*mani*-مَنِيّ), and one is considered to be *junub* or in a state of janabah.

Female ejaculation is the release of fluid within the vaginal canal that is a result of peak sexual arousal, having and resulting in the same preceding characteristics.

***fajr*** (فَجْر). Dawn.

***fatwa*** (فتوى). Religious verdict from a jurist of emulation (marja).

***fidyah*** (فِدْيَة). 0.75 kg of food for each fast day missed.

***ghaflah*** (غَفلة). Inattentive.

***ghayr muayyan*** (غَيْرُ مُعَيَّن). Unspecified (for example, making an intention to fast but not specifying the day).

***ghusl*** (غُسْل). Major ablution performed by washing (with water only) the whole body—either by washing every body part in stages from the head to the neck to the rest of the body (as one would have to do in a shower) or by immersing the whole body in water at once (as one could do in a river).

***hadd al-tarrakhuss*** (حَدُّ التَّرَخُّص). The point at which a person becomes a traveler based on religious criteria. It is the point outside the periphery of the hometown where the traveler is no longer visible by the people of the town.

***haydh*** (حَيْض). Menstrual bleeding.

## Glossary

***intercourse*** (دُخُول). The insertion of the head of the male penis into the vagina or anus such that the head is no longer visible.

***istihadha kubra*** (اسْتِحاضَة كُبْرى). Heavy non-menstrual bleeding.

***itmam iddah*** (إتْمام عِدَّة). The passing of thirty days of a month.

***janabah*** (جَنابَة). The state of releasing ejaculate by a man or woman because of intercourse, foreplay, a wet dream, or any other reason. Such a state requires ghusl of janabah.

***juma*** (جُماع). Sexual intercourse.

***kaffarah*** (كَفّارَة). The religious penalty to absolve a sin. It can be in the form of food, money, an act of worship, or other things (based on the specific sin someone may have committed).[28]

***maghrib*** (مَغْرِب). The time for prayer after sunset, when the redness of the eastern sky, which persists in the east for some time after sunset, disappears from above one's head when one looks vertically upwards.

***marja*** (مَرْجِع). Jurist of emulation.

***muayyan*** (مُعَيَّن). Specified (for example, making an intention to fast on Thursday); see also ghayr muayyan.

---

28. Explained in detail in I.M.A.M.'s publication called *Islamic Laws of Expiation*.

**mudd** (مُدّ). A measurement equal to approximately 1.65 pounds.

**mujnib** (مُجْنِب). One who is in the state of janabah.

**muqassir** (مُقَصِّر). One who did not make the necessary effort to learn religious laws.

**nadhr** (نَذْر). To make a promise to Allah that if He does something for you that you will do something in return. It must be verbalized in a specific manner: "*Nadhrun lillahi alay* that I do such-and-such if Allah does such-and-such for me."

**nifas** (نفاس). Postpartum bleeding.

**niyyah** (نِيَّة). Intention.

**niyyah irtikaziyyah** (نِيَّةٌ ارْتِكازِيّة). Formulation of the intention within one's consciousness.

**obligatory precaution** (احْتِياط وُجُوبِي). This is a ruling that is obligatory to follow based on precaution. According to Sayyid al-Sistani, in such verdicts, one may follow the next most knowledgeable jurist after him.

**qada** (قَضاء). Make up.

**qasr** (قَصْر). A shortening of prayers (by praying a specified fewer number of *rakah*). For example, a four-rakah prayer becomes a two-rakah prayer when traveling.

**raja al-matlubiyyah** (رَجاءَ الْمَطْلُوبِيَّة). An intention for an act of worship (e.g., fasting, prayer) that the jurist cannot establish with certainty that it is legislated as such by God (wajib); "hope that it is required by Allah."

# Glossary

***sawm qada*** (صَوْم قَضاء). Make-up fast.

***tawatur*** (ثَوائر). Widespread news from which one can obtain knowledge or contentment.

***tayammum*** (تَيَمُّم). A substitute for wudu and ghusl when water is unavailable. It is done by striking the hands on the earth and then wiping the forehead and the hands. With the inside of the left hand, wipe the outside of the right hand. Then with the inside of the right hand, wipe the outside of the left hand. For ghusl, strike the ground and wipe in the same way again.

***wajib*** (واجِب). Obligatory; legislated by God.

***al-watan al-shari*** (الوَطَنُ الشَّرعِي). Islamic domicile; a place that a person considers their home. This is either where they were born, where they live permanently, or plan to reside for ten days or more.

***wudu*** (وُضُوء). Ritual ablution.

***yamin*** (يَمِين). A promise or a covenant that must be verbalized in a specific way for it to be valid: "*Wallahi* (وَالله), I will fast tomorrow."

# Other publications from I.M.A.M.

## Available for purchase online

- ❖ Youth: Advice from Grand Ayatullah Sayyid Ali al-Husseini al-Sistani
  *Also available in Arabic, Farsi, and Urdu*
- ❖ Islamic Laws of the Will by Grand Ayatullah Sayyid Ali al-Husseini al-Sistani
- ❖ Islamic Laws of Expiation by Grand Ayatullah Sayyid Ali al-Husseini al-Sistani
- ❖ Islamic Laws of Food & Drink by Grand Ayatullah Sayyid Ali al-Husseini al-Sistani
- ❖ Shia Muslims: Our Identity, Our Vision, and the Way Forward by Sayyid M.B. Kashmiri
- ❖ Who is Hussain? by Dr. Mehdi Saeed Hazari
  *Also available in Spanish*
- ❖ The Illuminating Lantern: An Exposition of Subtleties from the Quran by Shaykh Habib al-Kadhimi
- ❖ Tajwid: A Guide to Quranic Recitation by Shaykh Rizwan Arastu
- ❖ God's Emissaries: Adam to Jesus by Shaykh Rizwan Arastu

www.ingramcontent.com/pod-product-compliance
Lightning Source LLC
Chambersburg PA
CBHW061335040426
42444CB00011B/2930